Mom's the Word

Mom's the Word

Conceived & Written by

Linda A. Carson, Jill Daum, Alison Kelly,
Robin Nichol, Barbara Pollard &
Deborah Williams

(The Mom's the Word Collective)

Foreword by Barbara Crook

Talonbooks
2000

Talonbooks
#104—3100 Production Way
Burnaby, British Columbia, Canada V5A 4R4

Typeset in New Baskerville and printed and bound in Canada by Hignell Printing Ltd.

First Printing: February 2000

Talonbooks are distributed in Canada by General Distribution Services, 325 Humber College Blvd., Toronto, Ontario, Canada M9W 7C3; Tel.: (416)213-1919; Fax: (416)213-1917.

Talonbooks are distributed in the U.S.A. by General Distribution Services Inc., 4500 Witmer Industrial Estates, Niagara Falls, New York, U.S.A. 14305-1386; Tel.: 1-800-805-1083; Fax: 1-800-481-6207.

 Canada

The publisher gratefully acknowledges the financial support of the Canada Council for the Arts; the Government of Canada through the Book Publishing Industry Development Program; and the Province of British Columbia through the British Columbia Arts Council for our publishing activities.

Canadian Cataloguing in Publication Data
Main entry under title:

Mom's the word

 ISBN 0-88922-431-5

 1. Motherhood–Drama. I. Carson, Linda A., 1958-
PS8309.M64M65 2000   C812'.6   C00-910151-9
PR9196.7.M64M65 2000

Acknowledgements

The Mom's the Word Collective would like to thank the following for their support:

Vancouver Women In View festival, Kenn Walker and the New Play Centre, Jan Hodgson, Joan MacLean, Susinn McFarlin, Hilary Strang, Annabel Kershaw, Andy Burnette, Ewan Burnette and all the Australian "Mums," Pam Johnson, Kathryn Shaw, Jane Heyman, Studio 58, Marion Ditrich, Liz Scully, Lynn Van Deursen, Kate Weiss, Mary Desprez, Donna Wong Juliani, The Vancouver Playhouse, Ray Wallis, Miriam Ulrych, Barbara Crook, Judy Richardson, Rob Richardson, and all our babysitters across Canada.

We'd like to thank our partners for their support, encouragement, and hard work: Bruce, Geoffery, John, Ross, James, and Kim.

And we'd like to thank our kids without whom we would never have had to write this in the first place: Julian and Timothy, Harlan and Hattie, Ben and Maeve, Lily and Finlay, Emma and Desmond, and Jeremiah and Georgia.

Special thanks to our families and friends for their support and generosity, without their help in everything from building the set, to watching the kids, to providing day-to-day inspiration this project would never have been completed.

Foreword

They were professionals in the theatre, but when it came to motherhood, they were rank amateurs.

They were supposed to be writing a play for a women's arts festival, but they were so busy sharing their deepest secrets and their perceived failings as mothers, wives and women that they didn't write down anything for almost a year.

When they finally scrambled together a show, they expected it to be over and done with after the scheduled four performances. Instead, they've performed their engaging play more than 500 times in Canada and Australia, and are about to share it with the rest of the world.

They are the moms of *Mom's the Word*: Linda A. Carson, Jill Daum, Alison Kelly, Robin Nichol, Barbara Pollard and Deborah Williams. The universal truths they articulate in this play have touched thousands of women and men of all ages—parents and non-parents alike.

"There's a level of honesty that people recognize," says Pollard. "The gray-haired grandmas come to the show and say, 'That's exactly how it happened to me— I've had that moment,' even though it was seventy years ago."

I had the privilege of reviewing the very first performance of *Mom's the Word* at Vancouver's Women In View festival in January 1994. As I wrote in the *Vancouver Sun*, "I laughed and cried for an hour, and I'm just a wicked stepmother."

No matter how many times I have seen the show since, or how well I have come to know the creators and their script, *Mom's the Word* still has the power to move me in a way that few other theatre pieces have.

The honesty of their sketches, anecdotes and "mom-o-logues" is what provokes the laughter and tears every time. That, and the appealing vulnerability of the writer-performers.

They don't pretend to be role models or experts, or to represent the experiences of all other mothers. They tell their own stories, no matter how painful or embarrassing, with such candour and vivid detail that even those of us who haven't given birth feel as if we know what they're talking about.

The title reflects the creators' belief that few women are willing to talk about what motherhood is really like, or to admit they're having trouble.

These mothers start where the parenting books leave off, and reveal what's really behind those manufactured media images of perfectly-dressed mothers, angelic children, doting fathers, designer houses and passionate post-partum trysts.

Real motherhood means leaking breasts, diminished mental acuity, depressed libido, the toxic sludge of fermenting diaper pails and the daily transformation of a well-intentioned mother from Mary Poppins to Cruella DeVil.

Fortunately, as the Moms hasten to point out, it also means falling in love with your child every day.

Sharing the good and the bad and putting it into words was the aim of the writers' support group Carson organized in early 1993. All of the women had worked in theatre—Nichol and Pollard as directors, the others as actors—and had husbands who worked in the arts. Each had one or two children under five. Each knew at least one other participant, but no one knew everyone—a situation that was soon to change.

They started each weekly meeting with a "check-in," a chance for each woman to talk about how she was feeling and what was happening in her life. Little did they know that these shared confidences, which included the most intimate details of their marriages and sex lives, would ultimately form the basis of their play.

"If you wanted people's attention for more than two seconds, you had to have something good to say," recalls Daum. "Maybe that's how it got so entertaining."

They spent more time talking than writing for most of the year, while Carson kept throwing out and retrieving the application for the Women In View festival. The heart of the play came together in the three weeks before the festival, as the six women cobbled together a working order and figured out which confessions were worth sharing with an audience.

Opening night of the one-act play was greeted by explosions of laughter, tears, shocked gasps and jolts of recognition. Nothing in the show was predictable, but every moment rang true.

"I think it was important that we were right there, living the experiences of the show and writing them down, instead of looking back on them a few years later," says Carson.

"I think that's where some of the really deep humour came from—and from the fact that we were not afraid to be completely honest."

Williams' squirting breasts, Pollard's nude streak across the stage in search of an errant child in a swimming pool locker room, Kelly's heart-rending stories of her premature son's fight for survival, Carson's angry "Dear Partner" letters, Daum's devious scheme for grabbing extra "sympathy sleep," Nichol's fear of leaving the baby on the roof of the car—these warts-and-all stories were also compelling theatre.

The standing ovation that greeted the premiere performance was to be the first of many. The Moms returned to the women's festival in January 1995 with a full-length version of the play, then produced the show themselves for a series of successful Vancouver runs.

Mom's the Word ran for eight months at Vancouver's popular Arts Club Theatre, toured British Columbia and Western Canada and won two Jessie Richardson Awards—the Vancouver theatre community's top honours—for best play and best collective creation.

They received scores of fan letters and had regular backstage visits from mothers eager to share their own experiences.

"A woman came up to me in Victoria, put her hand on my arm—I could feel her shaking—and whispered, 'Thank you, you have just relieved ninety per cent of my guilt,'" recalls Kelly.

"For the people who are in the throes of new motherhood, the show gives them a sense that they're not alone."

The original six appeared to have the show down to a science. They trained regular replacement actors to fill in whenever one of the Moms had family or professional obligations that conflicted with a gig. They never cancelled a performance, even if it meant going onstage with strep throat, after dental surgery or, in the case of one member, in the throes of clinical depression.

But success was taking its toll on the individuals and the group. Trying to be friends, castmates, producers and business partners, while juggling family demands, led to serious rifts and conflicts within the collective. Pre-show business meetings created tensions that weren't getting resolved. The honesty and mutual trust that had allowed the six women to share their innermost fears had all but evaporated.

"I would be crying so hard before I went onstage that I was not sure I'd be able to say the lines without breaking down," Daum recalls.

Adds Williams: "I thought I would always have hate—that everything we had had was just gone. I had these friends, and I needed them back."

So the Moms went to counselling. They spent a weekend in intensive individual and group sessions, and learned how to make their partnership work again.

"I had no expectation that we would come out of it as buddies," says Nichol. "I just expected that we would come out with a set of rules to follow."

But the "born-again" group members managed to rediscover their friendships as they rescued their professional partnership. As well as learning new "Quaker-style" meeting rules, in which each woman was allowed to speak her personal truths, the women learned to express and respect their own and others' feelings.

"During the counselling, we flashed back to that first year together, and how we had all laughed and cried, before we ran into trouble and started hating each other," says Carson.

"In counselling, we broke everything down again and started seeing each person as an individual, and it was quite amazing."

The next time success came calling, the Moms were ready. A man who saw and loved the show in Victoria, B.C., sent an audio tape of *Mom's the Word* to his brother, Australian TV and film producer Ewan Burnett.

Burnett brought the Moms to the Melbourne International Comedy Festival, where they did six shows in the spring of 1998, then turned the play over to an Australian cast. It was a huge hit Down Under, playing to sold-out houses in Australia.

Once the creators realized how well the play could work with other performers and for non-Canadian audiences, the stage was set for international success. Although the original Moms are ready to move on to other projects, they've signed a licensing agreement that will see the play performed in other languages and other countries worldwide.

The infants and toddlers who inspired *Mom's the Word* are now old enough to have seen the show and boast about what their mothers do. And who knows? They may inspire another show someday.

"We really want to write a show about teenagers," Carson quips. "We're screwing up our children's lives so that we'll get a really interesting show out of it!"

—Barbara Crook

Barbara Crook, former theatre critic of the Ottawa Citizen *and the* Vancouver Sun, *is a freelance writer and critic who teaches arts journalism at Carleton University in Ottawa.*

Mom's the Word

The original production of this script was first performed at the Vancouver East Cultural Centre as part of the Women In View festival January 26, 1995 with the following cast:

DEBORAH	Deborah Williams
BARBARA	Barbara Pollard
JILL	Jill Daum
ROBIN	Robin Nichol
ALISON	Alison Kelly
LINDA	Linda A Carson

Set Design: The Mom's the Word Collective
Directed by: The Mom's the Word Collective
Mise en scène: Kim Selody
Creative Consultant: Pam Johnson
Stage Manager: Jan Hodgson

Notes on Characters

These six women range in age from twenty-five to forty-five and are as diverse in their opinions, appearances and perspectives as one can possibly imagine. The actors must pull off the illusion that they are not acting, but relating a true story about themselves. They must be comfortable with directly addressing the audience. A keen sense of comic timing is a must.

ROBIN: Robin is practical, realistic, and down to earth. She has a dry sense of humour and takes no bullshit. She has a newborn and a two-and-a-half-year-old.

ALISON: Alison relates the stories of her premature first born in a clear and unsentimental way. Her life's experiences have in no way dampened her sense of humour. She has two children, a boy five years old and a girl two years old.

LINDA: Linda has the ability to commit 110% to both her quest to communicate and the ridiculous. She has two sons, aged two years and six months old.

BARBARA: Barbara is physically, comedically and vocally large. She has a one-year-old boy and a five-year-old girl.

JILL: Jill is a self-proclaimed bohemian who struggles with low self esteem. She was in her thirties when her first child was born. She has a boy and a girl, twenty-two months apart.

DEBORAH: Deborah is an edgy comedienne, who does not pull any punches with the bleakness of her stories. She has an infant and a two-year-old.

Act I

*Unless specified all the actors are on stage for the
entire show.*

Blackout.

Voices in the dark.

ROBIN:

You're not due for three months? My God you're
huge!

JILL:

You're five months pregnant? I have a friend who
miscarried at five months!

ALISON:

Never ride a bike while you're pregnant. You'll
tangle the baby up.

LINDA:

You're pregnant and you're going swimming?!
Won't the baby drown?

ROBIN:

Pregnant, eh. Are you constipated yet?

ALISON:

What's birth like? Pinch your upper lip. Harder …
Harder … Really, really hard … Now pull it over
your head.

JILL:

I heard giving birth was like having your leg sawed
off.

BARBARA:

Now that you're pregnant, I should tell you about the woman who had the forceps birth and the doctor pulled the baby's head right off!

DEBORAH:

Or the woman who went to the bathroom on an airplane and the pressure from the toilet sucked the baby right out of her!

Lights up.

Contractions Quickening

LINDA:

Contractions quickening—more intense.
Water gushing on admissions floor—we're here.
Aaah! Too busy! No rooms!—but we're here.
A room—a husband—a nurse?—maybe—yes …
Ouch! Gregarious! Too loud! Too jolly! But
forgiven, her heart is in the right place.
Our friend, a coach, glad she's here.
My husband—he's quiet, this is hard for him, but
he's there …
On and on.
Pain more excruciating pain.
Panic—pain—soft words—
Shoot the nurse!
My doctor, here, so quiet, soft, encouraging,
"Try the shower again, then we'll see"—"take each
one."
My nurse, "Do you want drugs? This? That?"
My doctor, quiet, "Just give it one more."
More pain, panic, failure, heartbreak. Can't give up.
Come too far. Body won't allow to give up!
No more please! But body has kicked in! Please be
over!
Nurse's hand to squeeze—I deliberately bite my
nails into it.
She is too loud, too confident, don't talk about
other stuff while I hurt!
Seems a week—only four hours.
Can I push? Not yet. Can I now? No. I want it over!
Okay push!

It hurts! The pushing hurts!
I thought it would be better, easier, gentler!
How? I can't!
Big nurse face blasting inches from mine, scolding,
instructing, yelling ...
Okay!
On and on.
I can't.
I cry ...
I'm no good at this.
A little head—
I see it—
Hard to keep looking—seems stationary.
Weak encouragement, "you're doing great."
I'm not though.
I know it.
On and on. On and on.
Until finally it starts to come.
Ooooouuuch! Skin stretching.
Gentle doctor, "Pant through it."
I can—I did!! It's happening!!
Great excitement in the room. Much different from
the flat "doing greats."
All excited ...
Push. The head—eyes up! Push. The shoulders!
The body! Such relief—flooding relief.
Such beauty.
The baby. So gentle.
Looking at his mama—his daddy—his doctor ...
his mama.
Such relief—
so happy—
so proud.
        She exits.

In the original production this piece as well as all of LINDA's letters were not addressed to the audience.

Ben #1

ALISON:

My baby looked like E.T. when he was born. He arrived almost three months too early. He was very sick, very little, and needed a lot of medical intervention to keep him alive. Moments before the birth, I remember my doctor warning me that I wouldn't be able to nurse him or even hold him, but afterwards, as the medical team whisked him away she said, "If you look quickly you'll see him," and a nurse running by held him up for me to see. A tiny two pound bundle. And when I saw him I felt love physically enter my body: deeper, stronger, than anything I'd ever known. And I knew that I would die for him.

Mom's the Word

In the original production everyone was in a line—looking sophisticated, business-like. All wore black trench coats.

Unless otherwise and specifically noted, women do not interact—they are busy maintaining their "cover."

LINDA enters in a rush, straightening out a dishevelled raincoat. She sees the others looking "perfect" and stops to sort herself out. She notices baby puke on her shoulder and tries to wipe it off. She can't. She sniffs her fingers and is disgusted at the smell. The women in the line-up secretly see and look away also in disgust. She carefully covers the section of her coat with her collar and takes place beside ROBIN at the end of the line.

LINDA:

(*notices audience and addresses them*) Oh, hi ... I'm really just a mom. (*reveals rat's nest of hair under hat*) I haven't been able to fix my hair for weeks! Shhhhh. (*replaces hat and returns to line-up pretending to be a business woman*)

   Pause.

JILL:

(*to LINDA and audience*) Psst ... I'm a mom too. (*reveals recognizable children's book under intellectual paper cover. LINDA and JILL laugh*) Shhhhh— (*return to neutral*)

   Pause.

BARBARA:

> Pst ... Do either of you have a cellular phone? (*to LINDA and JILL—reveals baby's toy phone from brief case. They laugh*) Shhh— (*return to neutral*)
>
> *Pause.*

ROBIN:

> Anyone else carry one of these? (*pulls out soother*)
>
> *BARBARA, JILL and LINDA pull out soothers and fool around while sucking on them. Everyone gets "caught" by DEBORAH and ALISON. Pause.*

ALISON:

> (*sings to herself*) The wheels on the bus go round and round ...

EVERYONE *(except DEBORAH)*:

> (*rousing*) ... round and round, round and round. The wh ... (*"caught" by DEBORAH—back to neutral*)
>
> *Pause.*
>
> *DEBORAH takes off coat and hat, steps forward, lifts dress, reveals breast and squirts milk. All are shocked. She turns and squirts others. Others get idea. Milk fight ensues with breasts and bottles. LINDA gets carried away and heads for audience, breast at the ready.*

EVERYONE:

> LINDA!!!

LINDA:

> (*to audience member*) Sorry ... (*all skulk back into line except DEBORAH*)

DEBORAH:

> (*to audience*) I saw you judging.
>
> *Segue into next piece—DEBORAH's "I Was a Woman."*

I Was a Woman

DEBORAH:

I was a woman who raised her eyebrows at mothers who raised their voices at children who raised their hands grasping for sugar from a cart.

I was a woman who thought disdainfully of mothers who plugged endless coins into motorized elephants, plugged soothers into slug-crossed faces, plugged babies into video-sitters.

I was a woman who judged mothers who smacked bottoms for the last misplaced headbut at the end of a long day.

I was a woman who internally "tched" at mothers, who had a beer while they nursed,
who used cookies as rewards,
whose children looked like dirt magnets,
who left the kids in the car while dropping mail in the box,
who put their child in daycare,
who hadn't put their child in daycare,
who lost interest in their careers,
who couldn't put themselves together in the morning,
who'd really let themselves go.

I was a woman who wasn't a mother.

I Used to Say

ROBIN:

Now, I always used to say that I wasn't a feminist because I didn't need to be. You get what you ask for, and if I expected to be treated "equally," I would be. I also always used to say that, on the whole, I didn't particularly like women very much. I much preferred the company of men. And I hated those things about myself that were stereotypically "female"—you know like irrational emotional reactions, the desire and ability to knit … stuff like that.

Then I got pregnant.

I really hated it. I couldn't escape those things about myself that were stereotypically "female." The most inescapable fact about me every minute of every day was that I was female, and my body was doing the most female job on earth. Women would come up to me in stores, on the street, … anywhere. They wanted to tell me their stories, they wanted to comment on my development. They wanted to touch me. It was like they wanted me to join this giant club.

What is the big deal about this shared experience? I'd been sharing the experience of menstruation with these same people for twenty years, but that hasn't been cause for this group hug with the sisterhood.

I'm not going to be one of those women who sits around all day gossiping and talking diapers. I'm not going to live in shopping malls, and I'm not going to watch hours and hours of daytime TV. Just because I'm going to have a child doesn't mean that it's going to change who I am. And it certainly doesn't mean that I'm going to suddenly have anything in common with other women.

Then I gave birth.

And I'm a member of the giant club. I see women on the street with babies and I feel like I understand them. I see mothers with two-year-olds having tantrums in grocery stores and I catch myself smiling with my lips together and my head on one side in that "I've been there" kind of way. I pass another stroller on the sidewalk and we give each other the high sign like two Harley riders passing on the open road …

So I guess I'm a feminist now. And now that I am a member of this club, I move that we have more parties.

Transformation

JILL:

Before I became pregnant I was what I would call
an urban woman. I attended all the openings,
galleries, theatres, dance, opera. I watched foreign
films galore—art house flicks. I read reviews of
books before I decided which author to next
explore. I watched bands in clubs while I drank
imported beer. I drank cappuccinos in coffee
shops, and when I ate, I ate in restaurants. Tiny
portions and large glasses of wine. I earned my
living from my art, "my work," which I discussed at
great length.

And then I became pregnant and everything
started to change. What I wanted to do most was
listen to my body. What did it need? What was that
tiny life inside me doing? I needed quiet to hear. I
began wanting to stay home to nest. Home. That
place where previously I'd only slept and selected
outfits from. My baby grew and I grew. I'd rub oil
on my belly and sing. I watched for bodily
secretions, colostrum, changes in discharge. And I
liked to sit for long periods of time not doing
anything—just feeling the wrigglings within.

And then came the birth. My breasts swayed as I
rocked on all fours growling and moaning. And
with a sound like I had never heard before, I
birthed my baby. My amazing perfect baby, who
sucked at my breast like a cub or calf. I spent weeks
not wanting to do anything but be near him. I had
to rely on my senses and my intuition for his

survival. I was bleeding, leaking breast milk, covered in spit-up and I hadn't washed or changed my clothes in days. I was no longer urbane. I had no desire to be. I was an animal. A proud, protective beast with a mother roar.

In the original production this piece was accompanied by a sequence of five slides—a city scape, a pregnant belly, two of a birth in progress, and JILL with her newborn.

Diaper Soup

BARBARA:

I wish I had known when I was in university that I would be spending the top earning years of my life cooking diaper soup in the basement. I might have diverted, oh, even one of my courses towards those more primary requirements in life. I mean I complain all the time about being over-worked and under-paid, but last week, after a particularly nasty splash emptying the diaper pail, I finally decided to do something about it. Actually I lie, it wasn't the diaper pail I was emptying at all, but rather the pre-soak pail. This is a system my husband dreamt up because he's not fond of rinsing poopy diapers in the toilet. He prefers to put them straight into the pre-soak pail where they float clean. It was an innocent trip down to the laundry room when suddenly the pre-soak pail caught my eye and I knew it had been forgotten. With trembling hand I reached for the lid. WHOA!! I deduced from the overwhelming evidence of a thick brown sludge gurgling on the top that it had been fermenting happily next to the furnace for a full ten days. I dragged the stinking cauldron across the room and managed to lift it just to the lip of the laundry basin where, with a monstrous impetus of it's own, it flew forth and I found myself facing an angry brown tidal wave. Luckily I had my glasses on that day because a tiny brown meatball trickled slowly down one lens. I did what I had to do. I marched straight upstairs, got on the phone, and phoned the sewer department. I wanted to find out what they earn, what my efforts were worth in the real world. If I'm going to work in a sewer I might as well be paid for it. I mean what the hell I've already got the uniform. I'll bring my own rubber gloves.

Mushbrain Song #1

LINDA:

Please excuse me?
I have mushbrain.
And it's not just hormones, no sleep,
or ... or ...
...

She completely blanks.

... Oops.

Time—A Poem

ALISON:

    There is a chair.
    Do I dare?
    Is there time?
    Time to sit?
    To relax?
    Too much to do.
    Always so much to do ... the cooking, the washing,
    the shopping, the cleaning up, the mopping up,
    the putting up, the shutting up ... of me.
    I must find more time to play with them, answer
    their questions, laugh, sing songs, look at their
    beautiful faces, their perfect bodies
    ... right after I've done the dishes.
    And there is that chair.

    I sit in that chair and I won't get up, my brain in a
    holding pattern.
    I sit in that chair and I become it, heavy, thick,
    inanimate.
    I sit in that chair and I vanish ...
    Is a moment too long to vanish?
    To think a thought through to the end?
    Time.
    It has a whole new meaning now.
    Sometimes so fast—
    TICKTOCKTICKTOCKTICKTOCK
    I can't possibly get it all done.
    And sometimes so slow—
    tiiiiiiiiiick toooooooooock.
    A whole day to go through.

Mushbrain Song #2

LINDA:
Oh! I remembered!
(*forgets again*)
Sorry.

Back Pack

DEBORAH:

My children have had a number of near-death
experiences, but my favorite happened downtown *
at rush hour.
I was taking the baby and putting her into the back
pack and I swung it up onto my back and she just
kept going. (*scream*) She landed on her head on
the cement five feet down. (*scream*) I couldn't stop
screaming.
I finally got us to the hospital.
Where they rushed us into the x-ray lab.
They gave us each a lead apron.
Clamped her head in place,
and told me to hold her down,
while she screamed louder than she did when she
hit the pavement.
And they said, "Don't let her move a muscle or
we'll have to do this all over again."
I knew right then that my life was going to change.
I'm going to have to give up my career,
but I will do that gladly as penance for what I've
done to you.
I'll push your little wheelchair around,
and teach you how to communicate on a spell
board,
make sure you get riding therapy on Thursdays,
and the house is going to have to be completely
re-done,
with ramps up to the front and back door,
and a big handle and a lift for the bathtub,

but we'll probably lose the house because of the bills.

But my family is going to rally round and ...

ROBIN *(as DOCTOR)*:

"Mrs. Williams?"

DEBORAH:

... make sure you have a vital, important, exciting—

ROBIN *(as DOCTOR)*:

"Mrs. Williams? Your daughter's going to be just fine."

DEBORAH:

What am I going to do with my life now?

    * Feel free to substitute specific local references.

Mushbrain Song #3

LINDA:

Ahhh!
Please excuse me?
I have mushbrain.
And it's not just hormones, no sleep, or breast milk
in my veins.
I live in this world
that is full of babies.
And my old world rushes by me too fast for my
mind to catch up.
Ta Da! (*bows*)

Books

ROBIN:

So, I recently had a baby. And this is the second time around for me, but since I can't remember anything that happened longer ago than last week, it's like the first time all over again. So the question is, do I really have to reinvent this wheel? Do I really have to go through this black hole of ignorance into the dawn of hard-fought personal experience again? Isn't there a short cut this time?

She is immediately deluged by the other mothers loading her down with piles of books.

Brief ad-libbing about the great usefulness of the books. Mothers begin to point out specific books and items in books.

LINDA:

(*indicating book about second children*) Someone gave me this for my second child. I didn't have time to read it.

ALISON:

(*reading from a book*) Here's a good one—"When you're having company over, just put the baby down two hours early so you can get ready."

LINDA:

(*reading from medical book*) Here's something: "Penis caught in zip. What should I do first? Don't touch the penis or the zip." Might be useful.

Gives ROBIN the book.

JILL:

> (*also reading*) What about this: "The basic cognitive unit is a concept that involves both mental organization and the child's conceptualization of a specific situation and observable behavior." No wonder I can't remember a thing I read in these books.

BARBARA:

> Actually I find it hard recommending books written by people who don't even have children. I'm just going to take a few of these back. (*begins taking books*)

DEBORAH:

> (*taking more away*) I have to admit I don't read any of them. I just read murder mysteries.

LINDA:

> (*taking more*) I'm just separating out the ones that I was too tired to wrap my brain around once I got the kids to bed.

ALISON:

> (*taking last of books*) My doctor gave me a great piece of advice. She said don't read the books. (*takes the last book out of ROBIN's hand*) They'll just confuse you.

BARBARA:

> You know I wish I had read somewhere how important it is to take your husband with you for the baby's first check-up.

ROBIN:

> Why?

BARBARA:

> He can't claim that he doesn't hear the baby crying in the middle of the night, if you get his hearing tested.

DEBORAH:

And a bit of a time-saver: Get the kids dressed for the next day before you put them to bed.

ALISON:

Oh, another time-saver: When you're cleaning up, instead of wasting a trip to the garbage can, just eat the food off the carpet.

LINDA:

Or, if you're driving and the baby's crying in his car seat and the toddler's screaming and throwing things from the back, I find it best to pull over, roll up the windows, get out, shut the door, and pretend everything is just fine.

JILL:

You guys, what do you think of this advice I got from my girlfriend: I was telling her about what happened with my three-year-old son and myself. He and I were having a day from hell; I just couldn't take it any more and I burst into tears. Well it was incredible what happened. He instantly transformed. He stopped finger painting with his lunch and he came over to me very concerned. He put his arm around me, he started to pat my back, and for the rest of the day he was an absolute pleasure. So I was confessing to my girlfriend that if things get really out of hand again, I just might use tears, and she said, "Oh yeah, I used to do that too, but you know what I found that works even better? Pretending you're dead."

All indicate agreement with this method or eagerness to give it a try and return with books to seats.

Letter #1

LINDA:

Dear Partner,

I miss our old relationship. We used to be two
people out there, in the world, doing our own
thing and coming together over romantic dinners
to discuss our days ...

And now you're out there in the world ... and I'm
at home with our baby ... and there are no more
romantic dinners.

You don't seem to have a clue about what my days
are like, and worse—you don't seem all that
interested either. But it's important to me that you
do know because ... this is half your world too!

Love, Linda.

Car Seat

ROBIN:

I have put my daughter into her car seat so many times that it has become a completely automatic, unconscious manoeuvre. It's now got to the point where I have panic attacks when I'm driving because I can't remember whether I put her in there or not and I have to do the quick shoulder check. To see that she's there. That I didn't … leave her with my coffee on the roof.

Preschool Women

JILL:

I take my son to this community centre, for a kind
of pre-preschool class. The first day that I took him
there, I found out that the parents weren't allowed
in. We were supposed to wait in this nearby room
in case we were needed. I had my younger
daughter with me and when we walked into this
room, I wasn't acknowledged at all by the other
mothers, who were waiting with their children's sib-
lings. So we just sat to one side. Now these women
all seemed to know each other. They were sharing
coffee and muffins, and they were all really well-
dressed, in these clean, coordinated outfits,
with hairdos and make-up, and their kids were
immaculate. We had to leave in such a hurry that
morning that I hadn't even brushed my teeth yet.
And my daughter, who was still in her pajamas, kept
gravitating to their side of the room. She was
attracted to their children's toys. I hadn't brought
anything to amuse her and she was tired of playing
peek-a-boo with a diaper. So I had to keep going
over to retrieve her, and each time I was met with
no response. I was starting to feel more and more
insignificant, so I began saying things to myself to
make myself feel better. You know, things like:
You're okay. You have friends. You used to have a
relatively successful career. You're married to a man
who loves you. He loves you. You're okay even
though these women are acting like you don't exist.
And it was just then that I thought—wait a minute.

We're all mothers. Which means we've all gotten pregnant, carried a baby, and birthed. And all of a sudden I was overcome with this urge to say, "Hey girls! Remember this one? AAAOWGHOUUANGHA!" *

* *Simulated loud childbirth appropriate noise, possibly delivered on all fours.*

Letter #2

LINDA

Dear Partner,

The world of motherhood seems so trivial. You
come home and say, "How was your day?" and I say,
"Well, I fed him and I changed him and I dressed
him ... then I fed him and I changed him and I
dressed him and we went for a walk, but he cried so
I had to carry him and push the stroller and ..."
Already I can see your brain racing for an escape to
something more interesting. So I quickly change
the subject: "What about your day?" But as I'm
listening I want to say, "Wait! Stop! Let's go back.
Much more happened in my day too! There ...
there was this look between us as I changed that
diaper. There was ..." I live all day in this world of
few words! How can I communicate to you what
that day is like?

Love, Linda.

* * *

ALISON:

I am such an idiot. I keep doing it. Taking the kids to restaurants. (*she exits*)

* * *

JILL:

> My two-year-old daughter has been having trouble
> sleeping lately, so I have been up for hours in the
> middle of the night singing lullaby after lullaby ...
> Usually ending up with the old standard: That's it!
> I've had it! GO TO SLEEP!!!!!

Sick

DEBORAH:
   I'm a fabulous mother when my kids are sick.
   Crisis.
   Everything else falls away and it becomes
   temporarily clear what the most important things in
   my life are.
   My babies.
   They're demanding but weak.
   Glistening and flushed with fever.
   Smelling slightly off-sweet.
   We sit all day with a puzzle and a book. I catch the
   vomit gratefully in my shirt.
   Change our clothes and the bedding, plump
   pillows.
   Ginger-ale to settle the stomach
   Cool clothes for the fever.
   And maybe just a touch of Tylenol and they're off
   again.
   Unconscious for four hours.

Shh Shh Shh

*ALISON enters with an infant car seat and diaper
bag, having added an oversized t-shirt and slippers.
Jiggling rhythmically.*

ALISON:

Shhhhhhhh Shhhh Shh Sh Sh (*three times*). I'm
trying to get her to sleep. She's almost there—I just
have to keep doing this and talking quietly. I'm
obsessed with sleep these days—her sleep or lack
thereof, my sleep and very much lack thereof, and
my five-year-old's sleep and how to convince him
that 5:30 in the morning is a really bad time to
wake up ... "Bad" is too strong a word isn't it? I
worry about using words like that and how they'll
affect him, and how much therapy he'll need if I
do use them ... Where was I? Oh yeah, I feel like
shit. Well look at me. A shower would be a luxury
right now. And I think I'm losing my mind. I went
to the door the other day, and I wondered why the
postie gave me such a funny look and then I
realized I had no skirt on. And how am I supposed
to resume a sex life when I wear a nursing bra. Of
course it comes off but then I'm a walking milk
fountain with no shut-off valve. There she's asleep.
(*puts down car seat—keeps jiggling*) Isn't she
beautiful? And smart. And I tell her that too. I
know it's important that she knows she is valued for
something other than her looks. Just like I tell my
five-year-old that he is handsome and gentle or
smart and sensitive.

*Has been hurling things out of the diaper bag while
searching for and finally finding a small doll. Puts
in the bucket with the baby. Sees the mess created by
the search through the diaper bag—unconsciously
stops jiggling.*

You know, I don't think of myself as a particularly
anal person, but now that I'm a mother I long for
order and routine in my life. I know I would be a
better person if I was more organized. A better
mother if I had lists of craft ideas I could resort to
happily and promptly on rainy days. My children
would grow to be well-adjusted adults if they had
days filled with routine balanced with a healthy
amount of free play. If I was more organized, I'd
never run out of diapers because laundry would be
done on a schedule. I'd never be caught with food
goo on my shirt because I'd always have a spare one
tucked neatly in my purse. I'd never ever forget the
diaper bag, always have the right things on hand to
whip up nutritious meals because groceries would
be done on a schedule, too. My children would be
perfect, I'd be witty, forget nothing, be able to have
a career and a clean home, sew a new wardrobe
with every passing season, plan perfect parties,
attend perfect parties, have a perfect marriage, be
able to speak my mind in a non-threatening, non-
confrontational manner, stop wars, feed the
hungry, and no child would ever be mistreated
again—ever ... Okay, so maybe I am expecting a bit
much. But those last three things, I want them. I
feel sort of responsible for all children now that I
have my own. I'm sorry. I'm becoming maudlin. I
cry at the drop of a hat and please don't tell me it's
hormones. (*bursting into tears*) Oh shit, she's awake

again. (*picks up car seat, resumes jiggling*) Shhhh Shh Sh Sh ... At least I've got my skirt on.

   Exits.

Letter #3

LINDA:

> Dear Partner,
>
> My day.
> A Poem.
>
> Warm enough?
> Soggy diaper. I'll wait 15 minutes, maybe he'll poo.
> "It's a hand! A hand! See? I have one too! A
> haaaaaaaaaaaaaand!"
> A long look between us as we share a bowl of cereal.
> So cute snuggled among his teddies on the couch.
> I'm sleepy.
> Coffee. (*look at clock*) It's only 9:15!
> Quick! Get the diaper bag packed fast.
> Ducks! We'll go feed the ducks!
>
> Love, Linda.

> *She exits.*

Shit

ROBIN:

Now, I have a mouth, as even my dear friends will tell you, like a truck driver. I was brought up in a home where taking the Lord's name in vain was a daily occurrence, and I have widely embellished on that since.

So, one day we're in the backyard discussing a tree being decimated by tent caterpillars and my daughter, two years old, points to the tree, big smile: "Looks like shit." Now we all know whose fault this is. And we all know how big this is going to go over with the in-laws to whom it's already had to be explained that she's talking about the truck, she just pronounces it with an "F." Obviously my act is going to have to become cleaner.

You know, I quit smoking four months before I got pregnant. I haven't had a hangover in years. I eat healthier, I go to bed earlier, I drive safer … Just how much more am I going to have to give up?

Day in the Life

DEBORAH

It always happens when I have to be somewhere on time and looking good and I'm not and I don't and on the way home one of them gets a nose bleed while the other one sucks on the germ-encrusted hand rails of the eastbound skytrain* and the connecting bus is late because of some fucking accident and I have to walk across the bridge during rush hour with one baby strapped to my body and the other one in some god-damned $15.95 stroller with one wheel that goes g-flap g-flap and twenty-five pounds of wet diapers on my back while the two-and-a-half-year-old whines: "Mom Mom Mom Mom Mom Mom Mooooooooooooooom." So we're home and it's dinner where he picks out every shred of grated zucchini and flicks it on the fridge and I remember he's probably not hungry because he had a tube of toothpaste earlier in the day. So it's bath time where they wait for all the water to run out before they get soaped up and I'm naked now because I refuse to change for a fourth time only to have my clothes soaked in bath water, food, spit, snot, blood, vomit, urine, or feces, and they find a four-day-old cup of V-8 juice and dump it in my lap.

"Jeremiah, Georgia, Mommy's angry ... and it's not at you. Go outside."

I start out Mary Poppins but I end up Cruella de Vil.

Use specific mass transportation reference for location of current production.

54

Hose

BARBARA:

It was spring. The first evening we could be outside without our coats on. I started puttering around the garden. Then I got out the hose and right away the kids wanted to get involved. That was fine. The little guy was too small to squeeze the nozzle and get any water out of it but his big sister was going to help him and that was great, but I was cautious. (*crouching, talking to child*) "Now Emma, you're just getting over your cold and your brother still has one so you can play with the hose, just ... don't get wet." (*small voice*) "Yes, Mom." Well, I just turned my back when all of a sudden I heard, "WAAAAAAAAAA!!!" I looked and there was a stream of ice-cold water blasting into my son's ear and my daughter was standing there with the hose in her hand and this maniacal little smirk on her face.

Well I lost it. I grabbed the hose out of her hand, pointed it right in her face and I said: "EMMA. HOW WOULD YOU LIKE IT IF SOMEONE BLASTED YOU IN THE FACE WITH ICE COLD WATER?" And she said: "YOU DON'T LOVE ME ANYMORE. I WISH I'D NEVER BEEN BORN!" and she ran screaming into the front yard. and that's when I saw my neighbours. They were sitting on their deck. With candles. And wine. And company.

Five minutes later my daughter and I were wrapped up together in forgiveness, and I thought—Why can't they see this? Anger is so loud and love is so quiet.

Angry Moms

"Angry Moms" is based on a clown exercise for the stage. The clowns are genuine, real characters and play at 100% energy. The trick is to be big and honest, yet never pushed or fake. In this piece, instead of being 100% "happy" the clowns are 100% mad, mean, and despicable. They threaten the audience and each other. They are dressed in raggy old dressing gowns, bare legs, with something from the baby world on their heads like small tights or plastic pants. They carry such household weapons as wooden spoons, potato mashers or small toilet plungers. The piece is done to a primitive chant and stomp. Enter ALISON and LINDA.

BOTH:
   AHHHHHHHHHHHHHHHHHH!

   Actors stomp about the stage intimidating audience.

Hugga, hugga, hugga, hugga,
Hugga, hugga, hugga, hugga,
Hugga, hugga, hugga, hugga,
Hugga, hugga, HUGGA!

   Actors come together to chant the following.

We are the angry Moms,
By golly by gum,
We're sick of wiping slime
From a baby's behind.
We are the angry Moms,
By golly by gum,

We want to vacuum the poop
Right out of their bums!
The individual lines are done simultaneously.
Actors break off on their own.

BOTH:
Hugga, hugga, hugga, hugga.

ALISON:
Come here and I'll give you something to cry
about!

LINDA:
(*pounding on her chest like Tarzan*) Aha, aha, aha,
aha, aha, a hugga!!

ALISON:
Wait 'til your father gets home!

LINDA:
Hugga, hugga, HUGGA!

BOTH:
Hugga, hugga, hugga, hugga.

ALISON:
AHHHHHHHHHHHHHHHH!

LINDA:
Hugga, hugga, HUGGA!
Actors come together.

BOTH:
Hugga, hugga, HUGGA!
We are the angry Moms,
By golly, by goo,
We no longer want to know
That cows go moooooo.
We are the angry Moms
By golly, by gee,

Just leave us alone
While we have a PEE!!!!!!!!!!!!!!

AHHHHHHHHHHHHHHHHHHHHHH!!!!!!!

Hugga, hugga, hugga, hugga,
Hugga, hugga, hugga, hugga.

> *Both exit.*

* * *

DEBORAH:

Every once in a while I realize I'm not teaching him enough and I panic: "Jeremiah! CIRCLE, CIRCLE, SQUARE, SQUARE. We've got to get this by LUNCH!"

Quake at Night

JILL:

At night after I finally put my two children to bed, I
quake. Like you would after a narrowly-avoided car
accident. You know the kind, where you have to
pull over to the side of the road and you just sit
there and tremble? It's because each day is filled
with one potential danger after another, and I'm
the one who must foresee and prevent every life-
threatening possibility. In the house alone you
have:

electrical sockets,
loose cords,
suffocation,
strangulation,
poisoning,
slipping,
scalding,
stairs,
pots on stoves,
faucets,
corners,
knives,
scissors,
fireplaces,
crib death,
choking,
burns,
sliding doors,
open doors ... then you're OUTside:
playgrounds,

falls,
concussions,
spinal damage,
broken limbs,
germs,
drowning,
communicable diseases,
car accidents,
child theft,
it's endless.

So at night, after I've checked to see that they're
still breathing, and I vow once again to sign up for
that Red Cross Child Safety Course, my knees give
in and I have to sit, white knuckled, until my pulse
quiets.

    Pause.

I made it through another day.

    ALISON and LINDA re-enter unobtrusively.

No

ROBIN:
Lily, no.
No, no, no, no, no, don't eat the plants.
No, don't pull the fur out of the dog!
No, we're not going to buy any candy today.
No, don't play with the answering machine!
No honey, you can't go outside now, it's bedtime.
NO MORE TOILET PAPER UP YOUR NOSE!

Do you want something to eat?

(no) *

How about some lunch?

(no)

Cheese sandwich?

(no)

Peanut butter and banana?

(no)

How about some Kraft dinner?

(no)

Try some of this.

(NO!)

Just a little bit.

(NO!!)

Just try a little bit of this.

(NO!!!)

YOU ARE JUST LIKE YOUR FATHER!

The "no"s in the second half should be provided by another actor on stage, from the side, as a voice only.

Ben #2

ALISON:

In the three-and-a-half months that my son lived in the hospital, my husband's and my daily routine consisted of waking up, phoning the hospital, eating breakfast, packing our lunches, and heading off to the hospital in time to catch doctors as they came off their morning rounds. One day we arrived to get the wonderful news that Ben's ventilator pressures had been dropped in the night. This meant three things: his lungs were getting stronger, he was doing more breathing on his own, and there was less chance of his lungs collapsing. We were elated—we were one step closer to having our baby home. I floated off to the pump room to express my breast milk, but upon returning to the nursery was told I couldn't go in. Now, this was no cause for alarm—it could have meant one of many things—a nurse changing an I.V., doctors consulting with parents, or doing more rounds. But I explained to the receptionist that I didn't want to visit with my baby, I just wanted to get my breast milk into the fridge, so she waved me on through. Now, to get to the nursery where the fridge was I had to cross through the nursery my son was in and as I did I glanced down toward his incubator to wave at our favorite nurse. There was a team of surgeons standing around his incubator: six doctors and nurses operating on a two-pound baby. The voice in my head told me I wasn't supposed to be seeing this. This is why they told me not to come in.

MOVE. But I couldn't. An intern observing the procedure came over and explained that both of Ben's lungs had collapsed. They would let us know something as soon as they could. I got my breast milk into the fridge, walked back through his nursery without looking at his incubator, went into the parent lounge, curled up with my husband, and cried.

The Other Man

BARBARA:

I'm falling in love with another man. And it's right
in front of my husband's face. We've talked about
it. I don't know, I was so busy and so caught up in
my work I didn't realize it was happening. But my
husband did. He was sitting right there, watching. I
mean there's this guy, this little guy, and his breath
is sweet, and his face is smooth, and he's promised
me he'll never ever grow whiskers on it. And I hold
him, and I kiss him, and I love him fiercely. And
one day I looked up and my husband was staring at
us with the most peculiar expression on his face
and he said, "It's a strange feeling to sit in the same
room with your lover and watch her fall in love with
someone else." But we know we'll be okay with it
because I'm watching him fall in love with our son
too.

I've Made a Mistake

DEBORAH:

It may be time to acknowledge the passing of post birth bliss when you look at them and the word "asshole" flashes across your mind.

I'm tired of being selfless.
Of giving my meal away one bite at a time.
Of reasoning when I want to scream.
Of understanding when I want to hit.
Of being ruled by erosion.
They're breaking my heirlooms and sucking me dry.
I want my life back. All of it.
ME MYSELF MINE.

I hate this. I hate them.

I'm tired of being a nag, a bag, a snag, a rag, for loathing every second that I'm stuck in this tar pit with them.

I've made a mistake.

Those wonderful gifts of life, those pink and blue snugly packages, have turned into writhing, squirming, kicking, biting, pinching, puking vermin.

This is bad.
This is permanent.

Confessions

This piece is played as a game of one-up-manship.

BARBARA:

Now that I have a family of my own I've never been happier in my life. And I've never complained more.

ROBIN:

When my two-year-old daughter bites some poor kid at the community centre, I don't make her say she's sorry. I just say as loud as I can, "Lily Nichol! What would your mother say?"

LINDA:

My family's favorite thing is to spend time all together. My favorite thing is to spend time all alone.

DEBORAH:

I find it much easier to be a good mom in public.

JILL:

Some mornings when I'm desperate for more sleep, I lie to my husband about how many times I got up in the night with the baby.

ALISON:

My fantasy is to be single, childless, and live in a really tidy home.

BARBARA:

Sometimes when I'm baking or whipping cream and the kids are in the next room? I don't call them and I lick the beaters myself.

Blackout.

End of Act I

Act II

Soap Box

ROBIN:

Welcome ladies and gentlemen to this the third in a series of lectures: "Motherhood Is What You Make It."

Now, you all know that being a mother is just one long endless string of life or death decisions that you have to make with either no help at all or enough conflicting advice to choke a horse. But of course you still have to make these decisions.

*DEBORAH:

Breast or bottle?

ROBIN:

Keep on making them.

DEBORAH:

Solid food? who, what, where, when, and why?

ROBIN:

Make more that are affected by the ones you've already made.

DEBORAH:

Preschool? Kindergarten? French immersion?

ROBIN:

Live with their ramifications.

DEBORAH:

Vaccinate or not?

ROBIN:

Or the threat of possible future ramifications.

DEBORAH:

Soother envy, nipple confusion.

ROBIN:

And if anything goes wrong, or appears to be wrong, or might soon be wrong, or is sure to eventually be wrong, Who's going to take it on the chin? Mom.

So. Who can these mothers turn to for some support in their times of trial? ... For some understanding and sympathy? ... For someone to help alleviate that standing-alone-in-the-middle-of-the-desert feeling?

DEBORAH:

Other mothers?

ROBIN:

Other mothers.

> *Giving cue for demo to begin. All directed at DEBORAH.*

BARBARA:

Still in diapers at four—how cute!

JILL:

(*to imaginary child*) Aw Johnny, did that little girl hit you? (*indicating DEBORAH's imaginary child*) Well I guess they don't practice positive conflict resolution in their house.

ALISON:

She's still not sleeping through the night? I never let my kids get away with that.

LINDA:

Not talking yet? My son's verbal ability developed so early. But they say it's directly related to the I.Q. of the parents.

ROBIN:

Those heart-stopping, soul-destroying judgements you live in fear of every day. They will not come from husbands, pediatricians, maternity nurses or even mothers-in-law. You have seen the enemy and she is right this minute saying:

DEBORAH:

Oh, you use a jolly jumper? We decided not to risk the permanent spinal disfigurement.

> *This is a lecture to the audience, perhaps a bit military in feel. DEBORAH is a "visual aid"—she is every mother demonstrating the to-be-expected responses. This is her first day and she takes her job very seriously. The other women are further aids to teach DEBORAH and the audience the lesson. It is important that their insults are veiled and their tone is helpful and friendly.*

Go Go Stop

LINDA:

Working.
Why do I do it?
Why do I even try?
Every time my ideas get going,
I have to stop and let them die.
My allotted time is over,
And I have to head for home,
But I want to keep on working.
My children for once postpone!
Go go stop. Go go stop.
I always hated that game.
Go go stop. Go go stop.
It would drive me insane.

But once at home makes perfect sense—adoring
children draw me back. To the beach I follow
toddlers and in that moment there's nothing I lack.

I know, I could quit working. Quit trying to play
that silly game. Swear off me forever. My ambition
finally tame.

As I vow, "Yes!" my work life emerges, and simmers
in my brain. Go go stop. Go go stop. Maybe I could
learn to play that game.

* * *

ALISON:

I used to have so much compassion for my husband when he got sick. Now all I can think is, "Oh great. One more person to take care of!"

Home

JILL:

> If only I had understood when I was younger what amazing things my body was going to do, maybe I would have criticized and mistreated it less and appreciated it more. The other night my husband and I made love and as we were lying together afterwards I had this incredible feeling that he was home. That we were meant to be this close and he had returned home. And then I thought about our two children and how they had lived and grown in me, and I had this sense that ... I am my family's home. I am home.

EVERYONE:

> You had SEX!!!

> *JILL reacts.*

ALISON:

> I haven't had sex for two months!

DEBORAH:

> I haven't had sex for eight months!

JILL:

> How could anyone not have sex for eight months?

> *ALISON exits.*

> *Segue into "Sex #1."*

Sex #1

BARBARA:

> (*bending from the waist, repeatedly picking up laundry and throwing it into a basket*) Oh man! Why am I the only one who ever picks up anything in this house. I swear to God if I went away for a week, we'd lose the baby!

PENIS PUPPET:

> (*one hand in the leg of a pair of baby sleepers, preferably with white plastic feet, the puppet speaking from the foot*) Helllooooo Gorgeous! I'm home!

BARBARA:

> What are you doing home so early?

PENIS PUPPET:

> I thought you might want to have sex?

BARBARA:

> I am doing housework! What put that idea into your head?

PENIS PUPPET:

> Not my fault. You bent over.

BARBARA:

> Why didn't I listen to my mother? Bend at the knees. Bend at the knees.

PENIS PUPPET:

> And sexy knees they are too!

BARBARA:

> This house is a pigsty and all you can think about is ...

PENIS PUPPET:

Your bodacious bum! You little sex monkey! (*she clamps his mouth, then lets go, but it's a warning*) Here honey, let me help you …

BARBARA:

I'll admit that the thought of you doing housework is about the only thing that could even remotely turn me on, but right now I'm wiped and I need my sleep!

PENIS PUPPET:

Honey, I'm just gonna go dust the bathroom and I'll be right back! (*PUPPET exits behind her back*)

BARBARA:

He's right. It's my own fault. Thirty extra pounds of flesh, nipples at my navel, greasy hair and big black circles under my eyes … I'm just too damn attractive!

Sex #2

ALISON enters wearing oversized t-shirt and mopping the floor—Mop ends up between her feet with the handle under her shirt at eye level.

ALISON:

Whoa! Honey! A surprise attack. That was fast. How are you? Well, I can see how you are … but I meant on a bigger scale how are you? You want to now—yes I can see that. Look, could we just talk? We never get to talk anymore. When was the last time you and I had a conversation about anything? You can't expect me to have sex with a stranger. Look, it's not you, it's me. I'm in demand all day with the kids and then sex just becomes another demand. So when you say you …

She steps forward causing the mop to droop.

I'm sorry.

Sex #3

DEBORAH is peeling and eating a banana—There should be no lewd physical indications of any other activity—She's just eating a banana—going through the motions. She speaks when she can between chewing.

DEBORAH:

Here, let me do this for you.

No, I know you'll never ask.

I don't get to do much for you anymore.

Because I want you to feel good.

Of course I feel good.

I feel good if you feel good.

She swallows, puts away any left over banana and sits down.

Sex #4

LINDA

(*lying on her side*) Oh! Yes I miss the cuddling too.
(*puts her nose in a book*) ... (*gets nudged from behind
and moves away*) Oh—Yeah, I miss the body warmth
too ... (*nose back in book*) ... (*lies on stomach*) Oh yes,
a massage would be wonderful. (*gets a poke*) Ahhh!
Get that thing away from me!

Crawls away fast.

Sex #5

DEBORAH:

I slept well, *Sesame Street* is on, the house is tidy, my mind is clear, you're at work.

I want to have sex now.

Sex #6

BARBARA:

(*as if in bed—blanket over knees*) Wow! Two nights in a row and the kids are asleep before ten! Did Desmond nap today?

PENIS PUPPET:

No.

BARBARA:

Great! Maybe he'll sleep through the night! You know, I'm actually starting to feel human again.

PENIS PUPPET:

Baby, you always feel great to me, and baby, the night is young!

BARBARA:

And so are you my handsome and virile young husband (*kiss*) mmmm ... (*PENIS PUPPET moans*) Honey, what is it? What's wrong?

PENIS PUPPET:

Gee—it's been so long—

BARBARA:

What? I thought you wanted to have sex?!?!

PENIS PUPPET:

We just did.

Mother's Echoes

JILL:

I've been doing some odd things lately, like the other day I heard myself saying to my daughter, "You're gonna get it." Get what? What was I talking about? And then I remembered saying, "Awww did you get a booboo?" Booboo? I didn't choose "booboo" to come out of my mouth. After that I caught myself stealing leftovers off my son's plate on the way to the garbage, and then I wiped his face clean with my saliva, and I thought what is going on? You'd think I was turning into my mo ... (*stops herself*) Nooo ... Nooo ... that's not possible. I've rebelled all my life. No one can tell me that all my hair dye, tattooing, and piercing has been for nothing. Just because I called my husband at work to ask him to pick up a loaf of bread on the way home, or stood at the back porch yelling at the top of my lungs, "Harlan! Hattie! Dinner!" That doesn't mean that I'm going to say ...

ALISON:

Let me push your hair back so I can see your beautiful face.

ROBIN:

Don't touch that, I just cleaned it.

LINDA:

Who took my good scissors?

ROBIN:

Don't wear that, I just washed it.

BARBARA:
Of course you can't find it, it's hanging up.

ROBIN:
Don't eat that, I just bought it.

JILL:
… I hope this doesn't mean I'm going to start ironing sheets.

Nursing

DEBORAH:

Nursing really is my thing. Maybe because it started out so badly. Neither of us caught on to it. So there we were in a breast feeding clinic with four adults trying to get a baby, with a name much bigger than he was, to latch on ... Latch on ... Latch on. It eventually worked and now I can't be stopped. I'm a nursing pioneer.

Sitting down, standing up, lying on my back like a sow—my breasts are long and flat.

In the bath, in the shower, in the pool, in the park—my nipples are soaker hoses.

While I dine, on the phone, while I pee, and I floss—you have to loop one end around your tongue.

On buses, trains, planes. Kneeling backwards over a car seat going ninety kilometers an hour.

In the forest, on a mountain, under the clearance rack at the Army and Navy. *

Inhibition gone, shirt open, rippled stomach bare, dress over my head, BREASTS A-BLAZING.

* Insert local bargain basement store name.

A Story About a Mother

ROBIN:

A long time ago there was a mother with two sons
and a husband. They lived on a farm in the middle
of nowhere, and there was always lots of work to do.
One day her husband left home to go and fight in
a great war and she didn't know how long he was
going to be gone or even if he was ever coming
back. She was forty years old.

Soon after her husband left she discovered that she
was going to have a baby. This made the mother
very sad and very scared. She didn't know how she
could possibly cope with the farm and her two
children and another baby all by herself. She
worried and worried about what was going to
happen and finally she decided that she had to do
something.

She stayed awake nights worrying and didn't get
enough to eat, but she was still going to have a
baby. She drank a special herb tea, but she was still
going to have a baby. She climbed onto the roof of
the sheep shed and jumped off, but she was still
going to have a baby. Finally, in the middle of a
very bad winter, and with her husband still away
fighting in the great war, her baby was born.

Afterwards the country doctor said, "I'm afraid I
don't much like the looks of this baby of yours."
The mother took him to an important doctor in
the city who told her that her baby was something
called a mongoloid.

Three years later her husband came home from the great war. Her older sons were men now and they went out into the world on their own. Her baby, who also grew to be a man, never learned how to talk, but he loved music, and she loved him. She, along with her husband saw that there wasn't much help for him in the world, so together they helped to establish schools, and associations, and group homes, and support systems, and one day they were given an award called the Order of Canada.

She dedicated the rest of her life to her youngest son, and she was very happy. And if she ever worried about the sheep shed, she never mentioned it to anyone.

Every week until she died, my grandmother drove to the school that she had helped to start and played the piano for the kids.

Letter #4

LINDA:

Dear Partner,

I usually write to knock down a wall of no communication.
To bulldoze through a road to understanding.
You know, I appreciate you!
My year of chipping away seems to have reached you, and into you, and become a part of you!
Surprise!
No complaints!

Love, Linda.

* * *

BARBARA:

When I was single I always used to worry about someone breaking into my apartment. But now that I have kids I don't give it a second thought, because I know no person could walk across the my living room floor in the dark without breaking their neck!

Missing Child

ALISON:

Making dinner while my children played in the next room, I drifted off into a thought. Coming to, I realized that things were too quiet. Checking the living room I saw my son engrossed in play, no little girl, and the front door wide open. We live on a very busy street. I checked the front yard—no child, the car—no child, the path to the park—no child. I could feel the panic coming up as I started running toward the park calling her name. Startled two women from their conversation, "Have you seen a little girl?" They haven't and the panic threatens to overwhelm me. Back to the house, between the houses, yell through a window at a neighbour, "I can't find her," on to the next neighbour—no one home. Back between the houses, checking garages, back to the park. Along with her name, sounds are coming out—foreign sounds, moans and sobs. My memory spits out the ghastly sound of a car door slamming in the silence before realizing she was gone. A man passing the house asks who I am looking for. "A little girl, she's two." A neighbour driving by sees my face and pulls into the driveway. "Have you phoned?" she asks. Into the house, I grab the phone but I am shaking too hard to push the buttons. She phones. I am in the rocking chair, holding myself, screaming sounds, can't see, can't breathe, can't sit still. I am up, running, screaming her name. Out onto the street. I see one of the women I yelled at earlier.

She is crouching at the end of the block, talking to someone small. Is it? A little leg appears—it's her!! I am running, crying, I grab her, cling to her. My legs give out. I shake for hours.

BARBARA:
(*spoken*)
Rock a bye baby
Safe in my arms
As long as I hold you
You'll come to no harm.

BARBARA exits.

Letter #5

LINDA

(holding a letter of many pages attached together—i.e. old computer paper—folded to the size of a single sheet)

Dear Husband, Dear Partner, Dear Father of our children, *(shakes out entire letter)*

Just when I thought you really understood! Just when I thought all my insistent, fumbling efforts at communication had really sunk in, you go ahead and make the bonehead comments of last night!— And when I asked you to apologize this morning you said: "For what?"

Ahhh! It all started late last night when you asked me to help you with the children and I said no. You thought I was taunting you, but I simply needed some time off. You said: "You never get any time off because you work so hard all day and then come home to 'hand over time.'" During my day with the children I don't get the choice of taking one moment for myself. With your work you do have the option. It's your choice not to take it. It's stupid to drive yourself all day with no lunch and no breaks. Especially now you have a family! We need you in reasonably good shape when you come home.

I cannot believe you said, "Looking after children should come naturally!" Who says? About as naturally as writing a symphony or learning how to juggle burning torches on a tightrope! Perhaps in a simpler society it was more "natural" but even then

I bet it was naturally hard work and many of the children died.

You have more responsibility than me? Wooo! You are dealing with a larger budget? WOOOOO! How much do you think our children are worth? What would happen if you got up and left your desk for four hours? What would happen if I got up and left the house for four hours?!!!

I know, I know. You do try and you do do a lot. It's a shame that our society separates our worlds so completely, but it is still my quest to communicate to you what my world is like so that you can be a part of it, be my partner in it, and not make comments that burn my shorts!

Love, Linda.

Aquatic Centre

BARBARA enters in bathing suit carrying a towel as if a child were inside.

BARBARA:

(*to child*) Wooo, that was fun, wasn't it? We went swimming didn't we?

She goes behind a barrier—only her head is visible.

Okay, here's our locker. I'll just get my key. (*fumbling with suit strap*) Oops have to put you down for a sec. Oh, stay here please. (*reaching to side*) Stay here. Okay! There we go! Oooh, chilly willy! Let's dry you off. Step out of your bathing suit please, step out, STEP OUT! There we go. Thank you. Now, let's dry your bum, your tiny, tiny, tiny, little bum. Now we need a diaper, diaper, diaper ... where is Mr. Diaper? Oh honey, don't touch that, that's not our stuff. You come here. Come on. Come help Mommy find Mr. Diaper. Where is he hiding? There he is! Naughty Mr. Diaper! ... Okay let's get your diaper on. You lie down. What have we here? Is this a tummy? (*tummy blast*) Ha! Gotcha! Okay. There we go, and a shirt ... that feels better, doesn't it? Nice and warm and ... Oh! Don't drink that. That's shampoo ... shampoo's yucky! Let's put the lid back on. No, shampoo is for washing your hair. We'll wash your hair tonight in the bath. Right now we have to go get Emma from school. And you're already dressed, aren't you? Yes. And now Mommy needs to get dressed too, doesn't she? Yes. Quickly. Here, sit down and drink some juice while Mommy gets dressed, okay? There we

go, you sit right there and drink your juice, that's a
good boy ...
(*removes suit—not obvious to audience*) God, I swear
this suit shrinks every time it gets near water. Oh,
honey didn't you like your ... ? Desmond? OH
SHIT! DESMOND! (*exits running, fully naked*)
DESMOOOOND!

Apology

DEBORAH:

I used to have a mind like the proverbial steel trap. It's just a trap now; nothing gets in, nothing gets out.

Half my brain washed out with my placenta and the rest is sloshing around and slowly draining out my nipples into my baby's mouth.

I've been told that it's temporary.
It's pregnancy.
It's hormones.
It's nursing.
It's those early years.

Anyway, (*begins to cry*) I just want to apologize that when I'm talking to you "grown-ups" I can't remember the point you're making.

Worms

ROBIN:

It was a beautiful summer Sunday and we were in the back yard trying to balance getting some work done in the garden with trying to keep our daughter from ingesting too much dirt. She was at that stage, you know, where everything she can get her hands on demands microscopic oral scrutiny, and she kept us petty busy. But the day was a successful one and the evening that followed was uneventful. Dinner, bath, bed.

First thing the next morning I was folding laundry in the living room and my daughter, who it is important to note had woken up moments before, was sitting on the couch sans diaper. Now that's a risky procedure, but we're under the hopeful impression that it will raise her awareness of her bodily functions and thereby bring closer that glorious time when ... but why am I torturing myself? So she was sitting on the couch and she was naked and I noticed that she was playing with something beside her on the couch. Something I didn't immediately recognize. I moved closer to investigate. I saw what it was. It, or rather I should say they, were two earthworms. They were warm. They were clean. They were alive. Where had they spent the night?

The Expert

LINDA:

I used to be an expert at looking after myself.

I remember thinking, my God I've spent thirty-five years of my life learning how to become an independent, self-supporting, stand-on-my-own-two-feet woman of the nineties, and suddenly I have these two little beings who are totally dependent upon me!

For a while I tried to find the words to keep myself connected to my old fields of expertise … But these days I think I am slipping farther and farther away.

I am becoming an expert at looking after my children. I am becoming dependent upon someone being dependent upon me. And what scares me most is my own resignation. My husband comes home to two noisy and happy children, and a very silent me. No letters, no lectures, no quests to communicate. Perhaps I have traveled so far into the land of dependence that when my babies get up and walk themselves off to school I will be left here alone, with no words. Too far from my old life to ever find it again.

I am brought from my reverie by two tiny arms wrapping around my knee and a burst of gleeful giggles, I bend down and pick up my baby, who is now a toddler, and hug him extra tightly.

Ben #3

ALISON:

Every day for three-and-a-half months we went to the hospital to do what little we could. Change a tiny diaper, take a temperature, take pictures, sing songs, talk to him—will him to live.

It was an emotional roller coaster. We clung to the highs of successes—"He's digesting one teaspoon of breast milk!" and waded through the defeat of illnesses—"He's had a brain hemorrhage." It was an education: learning to decipher the neutral faces and words of doctors; learning the medical lingo; learning what each machine, wire, and tube that he was hooked up to did. I have many memories of days that went on endlessly and yet some how sped by. But one day, "You can take him home."

"What! We're not ready. We're not prepared."

A sleepover in the hospital in a special bedroom to relieve some of the panic of being the only ones in charge. But during the night Ben slips back and has to go on oxygen again and we wait another five days. But then, as if none of the three-and-a-half months had occurred, I hold my baby, now just five pounds, in my arms. Quiet goodbyes to the doctors and nurses who are available. No chance to thank the hundreds of people who have been involved in this journey. We walk down the hall away from that secret, isolated world that has been ours. I glance over my shoulder, half expecting someone to come running after us saying, "Wait, there's been a mistake, you can't take that baby with you." But they didn't.

There have been many trips back. Hospital emergency rooms dreading hearing the words, "We want to admit him." Rushing into the hospital with a grey child limp in my arms. Two-day stays. Week-long stays. But we've never had to give him up for longer. He is ours forever.

The Gap

In the original production, the actress went into the audience.

DEBORAH:

I'm back.
I want that chair I left four years ago,
a drink,
and a long drag of conversation.
I'll inhale every word.

What did you do last night? What did you wear?
What did you say? No. You're so funny! Then what?
Please tell me! PLEASE TELL ME!!

I'm sorry.
I'm talking too fast.
I'm laughing too loud.
I'm sorry.
I'm just so glad to be here.
Am I looking too vicarious?

Your clothes are so nice, so neat and ironed,
and you smell so clean.
I'm pawing. I'm sorry.
I missed you.
Talk to me. Tell me about your child-free days.
Slow down. You're losing me.

Lost weight? Yes thanks I did.
I don't look like a mother?
Well if I don't open my mouth you'll never be able
to tell.

Oh my. I can still do this.

Well, you should have seen the colour of his Poopy-Poo!!

Silence.

This could take some practice.

Dresses

BARBARA enters with a dress box. As they speak, they each remove their dress from a rack, fold it up, and put it in the box.

BARBARA:
I used to wear this little dress. Opening night of the Stratford Shakespearean Festival Gala. Hundreds of guests, champagne, a live orchestra, and at one point everyone stopped and watched us dance.

JILL:
I bought this dress in Venice with my fiance, after a lunch of Chianti Classico on our way to an art exhibition.

LINDA:
Once a year my husband and I used to climb into the very same outfits as the year before, order a taxi, because we both drove scooters, go to a very expensive restaurant, and spend all of our rent money.

DEBORAH:
I primped, I fussed, I worried. (*throws dress in box*) I'm comfortable now.

ALISON:
With my hair up and high heels, I used to dance all night in this dress. Now I just look ridiculous in it. Besides, my bedtime is nine o'clock.

ROBIN:
I made this for my brother's wedding. When he told me he was engaged I cried ... I'll wear it again. (*returns her dress to hanger*)

Playground Gigolo

BARBARA:

We arrived at the park. There I was juggling stroller, diaper bag, bits of food, coats, hats, a rambunctious five-year-old and a very smelly little boy. My kids get so excited about going to the park that I always get sucked in to thinking I'm going to have a good time too. In reality it's a hell of a work out. I fantasize sometimes about being able to sit quietly in the shade with a fat novel, just to shut my eyes ... and relax .....

Music—dreamscape. In the original production this was created on a child's xylophone.

* CHILD'S CRY:
   MOM!!!!!!!!

BARBARA:

(*with heightened intensity*) Suddenly there's a sharp cry from my little girl. She hangs precariously from the topmost peak of the jungle gym. The baby squirms at my side, mid-diaper change, tiny penis pointing to the sky. I freeze in helpless frustration. (*one hand on baby, one reaching toward daughter*)

Music—"O Solo Mio."

(*looks over shoulder*) Suddenly there's a handsome young Mediterranean at my side.

* DEEP, SEXY, MALE VOICE:
   Por favor, may I be of some assistance?

BARBARA:

Well—I—My little girl! (*indicates daughter*)

MALE VOICE:

Would you allow me? … Have no fear.

BARBARA:

In a second he was at the jungle gym and with the prowess of an Olympic athlete he effortlessly plucked her from imminent danger. Winning her trust in an instant, he gently lowered her to the ground. Glancing at me for approval he whisked her onto the swings and before I could get the diaper bag repacked they were laughing happily together.

Music out.

What a wonderful man. And so handsome. I longed to thank him but the baby started howling with hunger. I instantly started nursing. (*mimes nursing baby*) My daughter I could see playing happily, but where was the handsome stranger?

"O Solo Mio."

Suddenly a cool glass of water appears before my face.

VOICE:

I thought you might be thirsty.

BARBARA:

(*to him*) Oh thank you, how sweet. Just set it down beside me and I'll have a hand free in a sec.

VOICE:

Por favor, allow me.

BARBARA:

> (*romance novel voice*) He held the elixir to my lips. A wedge of lemon swam tantalizingly before my eyes. I drank deeply.

VOICE:

> Señora, your shoulders look so tense ... May I? It would be an honour.

BARBARA:

> With the expertise of a professional he eased his thumbs onto my shoulders.

VOICE:

> You mothers are so wonderful, working like dogs night and day for nothing in return.

BARBARA

> My aching and sadly neglected muscles yielded willingly to his manly presence there. Again and again he thrust. Deeper and deeper and deeper.

VOICE:

> You give and you give and you give. You mothers should be sainted.

> *She sobs gratefully.*

VOICE:

> Senora, have I hurt you? (*she indicates not*) Madre de Dios! That little boy is going to fall! I must go!

BARBARA:

> And with a flash of his boyish grin (*music out*) he was gone. I sat quivering on the bench, a limpid form bathed in sunshine. A smile slipped knowingly from the mother opposite me.

> *"O Solo Mio" softly.*

* MOTHER 1:

> I see you've met Luigi. He taught my son how to ride a bike.

* MOTHER 2:

> As soon as it's warm enough, wear sandals—He gives foot massages.

* MOTHER 3:

> My daughter's first word was ...

* EVERYONE:

> LUIGI!

BARBARA:

> And I knew (*she stands, burping the baby*) I'd found a park to call home.

> *Music swells to finish.*

> ** The child's cry, the mother's voices, the music, and the voice of Luigi should all be provided by the actors on stage, the music preferably acappela. The voice of Luigi was created by two voices in unison.*

Thank You

ALISON:

"Thank you," the words I use when someone helps me as I struggle on the bus with two children, when my little girl paints me a picture, when my son gives me a kiss. What do I say to the people who kept my son alive? Thank you for life. The words don't match the magnitude of the event or my gratitude, but they are the only words I have. From the bottom of my heart, Thank You.

Miracle

JILL:

I will never lose my awe and mystification over my children's arrival. How all of a sudden at the end of labour, there was another person in the room, and they hadn't come in the door. They arrived … a perfect, glorious angel. Birthing is transcendent, painful, divine, and common. Each baby a miracle. But now I'm finding as my babies get a little older that sometimes their wings are hard to see. And other people's children? Well most of the time I can't see their wings at all. How is it that I don't revere every child I meet? And adults and teenagers, have they stopped being miracles? At what point in their life did that happen? And they became just that stupid slow cashier? That dumb driver in my way? Someone I hate? No, if you start out a miracle, you stay one. I am a miracle. And so are you. Someone's perfect baby. Maybe that's what I'm supposed to do. Never let my children forget that they're miracles.

Final Voices

ALISON:

The other day someone asked me why I had children. For me the excitement begins the moment they are born with, "Who is this person?" And everyday I get to see a little bit more of who those two people are.

DEBORAH:

My children have brought me so much laughter. I laugh with them, I laugh at them. They're wonderful entertainment.

BARBARA:

When I was a teenager I dreamed about being in love like this. I look at my kids and my knees grow weak and my love grows stronger every day.

ROBIN:

When people look at my children they say, "Boy, you can sure tell who their mother is," and I am overcome by the compliment.

JILL:

They constantly astound me. Their questions, their perception of the world, and their love.

LINDA:

Dear Partner,

My mother reminded me that these years are going to go by all too quickly. I suddenly thought of those obnoxious tourists who travel in exotic countries like Thailand or Brazil, and desperately need their bottles of Coke or rich western hotels. I have to be careful not to miss the rich moments of this voyage

I am on with a homesickness for a different sort of day in a different sort of country. I took the long flight into motherhood. I will live it.

In the original production we chose to augment this piece with two slides each of our children at the age they were when we wrote the play.

The End.